CRIPPLED DEMOCRACY
AND
OTHER POEMS FROM
THE FOOD CHAIN

BY S.E. MCKENZIE

ISBN-10: 1772810002

DEDICATION
To everyone who has been left out in the cold

THIS BOOK IS A BOOK OF SPECULATIVE FICTION
Characters, companies, governments, places, events, are either products of the author's imagination or used fictitiously. Any resemblance to persons (living or dead), companies, governments, places and/or events, is a coincidence and unintentional.

TABLE OF CONTENTS

CHAOS

CHAOS

I

Chaos; the ancient boss
When Hate and Fear
Are so near; calculate your loss;

In Chaos; the emptiness of Forever.

Forever
Good and Bad
A ladder

To climb

Into the beast's mouth

There was so much doubt;
Free Speech
For one;

To incite;
To fight;
All night.

Fate;
The change of the state;
Lost in the hate;

Those without power;
To speak the truth;
Feared Forever

The beastly mouth

Had taken over;
Now we must choose;
And still lose;
For the lesser of two evils;
A choice, not so great;
Feeds the fate of hate;

Anyway;
Could you stay
Awake?

For my sake;
Stay aware;
Of time;

The way; your fair share;
Of life is measured;
Will you stay

Until I understand
The line
That divides

But never multiplies?
Even when
A believer of True Love

Dies.

I see Fear in the deer
I see Fear
In your eyes

The Force leaves no disguise
For the Collective
To criticize.

How the Collective pretends
That it bends;
For all; not just friends;

How the Collective hides when it takes;
And conceals its mistakes;
Name plates left in a pile; identity is never clear.

Blurred by Fear
And tear drops;
When the decay they made

Never stops growing;
Showing; behind the door;
Is a troll;

We run when we see him stroll.

So safe
In our tree
Are we.

Though we cannot own our tree;
We
Are still free.

II
Predator
So willing to grant you a loan
Predator

Once in debt
You are partially owned
By another

Who will defy
When you ask
The truth

The Collective will lie;
So many stuck on the Pillory;
The watchers watch but cannot see;

As the Ghetto Queen
Laughs in glee;
The Nouveau Gestapo does not know

What he wants to be;
Used to be loved;
Now a stranger in a land

That he left behind.
Now;
Choose the turning points.

How the debt grows
Into borrowed tomorrows
As the Collective

Roll in their greed;
Create so much need;
Refuse to let go of the deed;
As the Troll
Has no money
To pay for the toll

The new bridge
Was built
Without a fight

On foreclosed land
New demand
New command

He looks for his prey
Everyday
He throws so many away.

Debtors insanity
Paves the way
As the Ghetto Queen laughs in glee.

The Troll
Looks for someone new
To balance his books

He looks; still stuck in a world so flat
And ready to oppose
Anyone who really knows.

How the grass grows
And how many on the other side
Stood their ground

As the Dinosaur lived Forever
In emulation
What a sensation

To build Forever;
A time no one knows how long
No reason to fight; just bask in the light

Inside; now out; turning points
Climbing into the sky;
So little room left;

Turning; Forever;

Leaving nowhere for the next generation to roam;
So afraid were their Mommas
When they left their home

To stray into hostile lands.

So afraid
Of loss to order;
Strung along

Chaos on the surface
Has reason and rhyme
As you climb

Into the sky; Fear Forever.

THE END

THE
DENOMINATOR

S.E. McKENZIE

THE DENOMINATOR

I

We go off to war
All of us
Together we are one;

Only numbers below the line.

We leave our homes and family
Hidden in mist
We hope we will be missed;

We fight
As we are told
We die before we grow old;
We are the numbers below the line.

Common denominator
That we all share; more than we dare;
Living below the line;

We ignore our fate;
We are shaped to hate
Whoever we are told

To hate; our hate
Makes us
Bold

Before we die
Never too old;
Never showing
Our love-lights never glowing;

For we are too cold;
We have grown
Without ever knowing love;

We are just part of the flock;
Who we could have been;
Will stay unlocked;

Deep inside;
We learn to hide;
What we hope could have been.

For we live
Below the line;
All the time;

Only a few
Will get away
Alive; most of us will stay;

In this grave;
For as long as forever;
For we must stay

Below the line.

Love has never been shown.
Love; the greatest value;
Always on loan;

For love
A greater force than you and I
A shadow we can only leave behind;

After we die;
We will grow
More loving and giving

After we die;
Part of we, will live in you;
Unconsciously; you know it is true;

Though the moment we die
No one will hear us cry;
We still wear our mask with pride;

Just a steely smile
Planted on our face; only place
Where we can hide.

From it all
Before we fall
Off the wall

We must guard;
For evermore;
For He lives behind its door;

II
When was the beginning?
We will never know;
We are just part of the flock

Ruled by his clock;

To remind us that our time;
Belonged to others;
Owners; not brothers;

We hold on to the dream;
We pass it on
Before the last scream

We cling to our vision;
Before we let go;
Of the rest of our life;

No crying we make;
We surrender to Eternity;
Which might just be

Another lie;
Maybe nowhere and nothing at all
Smaller than a spec on the wall;

That we guard before we fall.

III

We were told to never look back;
But I saw you looking back
Anyway;

Were you hoping
That the seed you had planted
Would have all your wished granted

So he could grow
Into tomorrow
Free from sorrow;

And remember you;
As the haunted ghost
Who loved him the most;

For ever more
Behind a closed door;
People fight for their last breath

Before they walk in.

IV

To grow up in the usual way;
Maybe even better than that;
A world of peace;

While the arms' dealers
Turn a profit
We are left out in the cold

Never allowed to grow old;
And were never to be captured;
That is what we were told;

S.E. McKENZIE

By a man
We would never know
Who lived in a tower

With a woman half his age;
Grew old fast with rage;
Would be replaced soon;

Just like us;
We climb the wall;
For a moment we feel tall;

Before the fall;
For the man in the tower
Had it all

And still wanted more;

But we
Lived below the line;
Time after time;

Our seeds were left
To live for us
The way we could not;

We would soon be left
On this battle field to rot;
We left our seed to grow

A precious life
Into tomorrow
Burdened by our sorrow

One more cycle in a knot again

Sometimes paralyzed in pain
Sometimes in love;
Soon to be swept into the heavens above

Or into the molten fire below;
We would never know;
If we could grow

A soul
Without having control
Over our fate

We try not to hate
He; who lives behind the door;
He who we guard

For evermore;

We grow into cycles
Spinning all around
One life ends

And one begins;
Bounded by time
Under the line.

THE END

CRIPPLED

DEMOCRACY

CRIPPLED DEMOCRACY
I

Born free no more;
Laws of Scarcity
Turning many into outlaws

Pushing even more out of the Door;
Feeling unloved and lost
More than ever before.

Miles and Mary held hands
Looked up into the sky
To see which way the wind would blow.

The game they were to play
Was sum-zero;
And nothing more;

No open door
To the Ivory Hall
They were stuck on the bad side of the wall.

Walking by;
Ghetto Queen sits on the steps
Outside of a Smokey private scene;

Reporting those who look suspiciously poor
To Nouveau Gestapo
Not in fashion when shopping at second hand store;

Soon someone Ghetto Queen never knew
Will have their back against the wall;
Could be me could be you;

But it was Mary and Miles;
While Ghetto Queen was buried in smiles;
Accusations fly;

So Ghetto Queen will have it all;

New world order;
Programmed to feel small
For ever more

Living on the bad side of the wall.
So Ghetto Queen can have it all;
On her side of the Public wall.

Integration;
Unknown complication;
Today; ignorance is bliss and cheap;

Dead bodies left in a heap;
Too dangerous
To think too deep.

II

Walls dividing
Haves from Have-nots.
Humans were under the influence

Of assimulated killer bots.

For ignorance was bliss and cheap;
Dead bodies piled in a heap;
Everyone was afraid to think too deep.

Ignorance was bliss;
For it was free;
Higher education was only for the mighty;

Demonization; new religion
For a dehumanized nation;
On the brink of perpetual war

So afraid to ask
"What are we fighting for?"
The walls squeezed in the town called Blue

Micro-managed to be so pure;
Everyone would reach heaven;
They were so sure.

III
We hid our minds in the sky

For Love was still hiding there;
Crying and dying; for Love could not belong
In a divided world where caring and sharing

Could not overcome greed and need;
Too many barriers inside a crumbling wall
No access to the Door to the ivory hall.

Complaint driven;
Evidence not needed to be given;
If you own it all.

Ignorance was bliss and cheap;
Dead bodies piled in a heap;
Too afraid of thinking too deep.

Two worlds;
One that raises the young to be mighty
Another diminishes the young until they crawl.

One side of the wall
Let's you stand tall;
Keep your head down;

If you are on the other side;
Ghetto Queen on a bender
With the watchers who cannot bend;

In the morning her head will hurt so bad
She will feel
It will never mend.

Mega rich guy
Will never have enough
In his world there is no need for love

So inflated; loves to talk tough
Never had to live rough;
His dream was to build a wall

Around every nation; needed no competition;

Monopolization
New world order
Chaos for those on the other side of the wall.

Tea is served for charity outside the Door
But won't serve you right
In their store,

Charity for the poor;
Thrown garbage;
Reselling it to the mega poor;

Degradation;
Lost in a dirty used world;
Progressing no more.

False accusations
Lapse in due process
Complaint driven

But no evidence given
Accept screams of pain
While the poorest of the poor

Are kicked down again.
Injury to the mind
Programmed from above

In a world with too little love
And too much hate
Inflating and negating fate.

Bait and switch;
Inflate the opportunity cost;
Youth is lost

Steely face of accusers;
Social abusers;
Sum zero game; no one knows your name;

Winners call us losers.

Miles Tory
Did not plead or beg
Was pressed and crushed like an egg.

Two days of torture
But Miles Tory
Knew his mind; did no plea;

Avoided forfeiture to big brother

Held on the best he could
So that we
From a supposedly gentler time

Would remember
Man's inhumanity to man
Never knowing when the hate began.

But lack of due process
Was not justice
At all;

Ignorance was bliss and cheap;
Dead bodies piled in a heap;
Too afraid to think too deep.

Look down the Ivory hall;
As far as you can;
Can you see a nobler man?

THE END

S.E. McKENZIE

FIRE

FIRE

I

Chemical change;
Hot Flames
Licking space

Too close to your face;

How did it start?
Some say from a spark;
Others say Fate;

Grew out of control;
Burnt everything in sight;
Fuel fed the Beast with all its might;

Fuel turned a spark into a giant;
Beast enjoyed the feast;
Toxic air everywhere;

Dreams up in smoke;
Fate's joke;
Some said Fate's due was untrue;

It was up to me and you
To add value;
To everything we do;

To measure the treasure;
A merchant's pleasure
No more;

Fire grew as it devoured fuel;
Fire's rage
Was in control

More powerful than the Queen's rule
Grew as it was fed fuel
Into a Beast no longer just a tool;

Fire was alive but not aware;
Fire could not care
As it spread dread everywhere;

II

Whispered lies
Needing no disguise;
Blocking ears to her silent cries.

Fire was all around
Scorched neighboring ground;
How did Fire start?

By a spark that was never put out;
Our minds were shattered as Fire grew into the Beast
Now we can only shout

"Remember to be true to your dreams

Especially now when shadowed by doubt;
Tearing so many lives apart
Fire did not know how it broke her heart."

III

The peasant king was wearing his crown
While he kept putting us all down;
For he had lost his smile

For he too felt
The burning sting
Of Fire.

King's face was burdened by his frown;
For Fire did not know Divine Rights
Nor Stakeholder Rights;

Fuel was all that Fire knew;
Growing from a spark
That could not die out;

Fire raged and burned down each door
As Fire kept burning it wanted more;
Fuel;

IV

We had No time
For higher learning.
We were left yearning

For those we left behind;
Now only the same
In name;

And nothing more.

We sit on this scorched Earth
Remembering its beauty; its worth
A long time ago, we stand brave

Only in vision
We had to make a decision
We stood at the foot of each new grave

We heard the sound

Of our strained breath;
For no sound came from the ground;
And we dared not to disturb those fallen

Into Infinity's sleep for evermore
Still connected;
We hoped they would be protected

For if they awoke
They would only weep;
Some say they are better off

In Eternal Sleep.
When one;
Unity;

Whole
Infinity;
No beginning or end;

Just a new way to bend
In the circle
Holding so many more

As flares from the sun
Warmed the snowball
Until it was partly blue

We all speculate
Before we stumble on a fact
Then there is no going back.

It is time to act.

V

One was not the first
Nor the last
Just the one

Without beginning or end
Infinity
Connected everyone

In one way or the other
We would always be
Sisters and brothers

Unity
In a land
That could never be free;

So much was predetermined
Once the spark ignited
Fire would grow to rule.

THE END

STRING

STRING
I

String a long
In this song;
Gravitation

Keeps us down on Earth;
We strum the string
We can't understand everything;

The switch;
The charge;
The Positive; the Negative

In every breath we take
We avoid massive implosion
While we harmonize.

Nature in all its forms;
Defying norms
Just to survive

The ocean comes in waves below;
Particles moving in the sky above; appear slow;
So far away and beyond comprehension;

As we gaze
We feel love
For the Heavens above;

Massive stars so far way
Flying above our graves in waves.
As Earth rotates away the day

II
Stability is lost;
When there is no motion;
There is no time;

For the signal to die;
Lost in the vacuum of the black hole
We cry out to Existence

Just for the love of it;
The beat of the Skin Drum
Drives life to come

As far as it can.
And how do we know
How far that can be

We are just mere mortals
And nothing more;
As we live beneath Heaven's Door

III

Our heart
Can only start
With a spark

So we took a walk
In the park
After dark

Hand in hand
We gazed into the sky
While particles moved

At the speed of light
We could only see this
Cause it was night

We assumed the right
To know the secrets of the Universe
Though we refused to believe

That there was a Multiverse.

IV

We live in this Sphere of Fear
No beginning or end
Light will always bend

For True Life
Must be round
To move

As we lay on this flat ground.

Our hearts
Kept tune
Under the moon

As the Skin Drum
Kept us alive
Our blood circulating

As one;
Infinity;
Connected

S.E. McKENZIE

To all we can see
And beyond
What some call

Divinity;
Life
Is all we know.

We bend the string

So we can hear it sing
For Harmony
Must be made

Then valued
For evermore
While we live

Under Heaven's door.
Like all the generations before
Our arrival

Our survival
Our revival
We live

For we have so much to give
Before we die;
Never knowing why.

We arrive in this world
Of the breathing
Crying

So afraid of living
And even more afraid of dying
We depend on love for we have nothing more.

THE END

Produced by S.E. McKenzie Productions
First Print Edition May 2016

Enquiries: 1(778)992-2453
Mailing Address:
S. E. McKenzie Productions
168 B 5th St.
Courtenay, BC
V9N 1J4

Email Address:
messidartha@aol.com

http://www.amazon.com/SarahMcKenzie/e/B00H9RWX48/

www.ingramcontent.com/pod-product-compliance
Lightning Source LLC
Chambersburg PA
CBHW060542030426
42337CB00021B/4388